D0560586

BOSTON COMMON PRESS
Brookline, Massachusetts

1997

Boston Common Press
17 Station Street
Brookline, Massachusetts 02147

ISBN 0-936184-18-3

Library of Congress Cataloging-in-Publication Data
The Editors of *Cook's Illustrated*
 How to stir-fry: An illustrated step-by-step guide to adapting a
Chinese technique to an American kitchen/The Editors of *Cook's Illustrated*
1st ed.


 Includes 35 recipes and 40 illustrations.
 ISBN 0-936184-18-3 (hardback): $14.95
 I. Cooking.  I. Title
1997


Manufactured in the United States of America


Distributed by Boston Common Press, 17 Station Street, Brookline,
MA 02147.


Cover and text design by Amy Klee

# HOW
# TO
# STIR-FRY

An illustrated step-by-step guide
to adapting a Chinese technique to an
American kitchen

## THE COOK'S ILLUSTRATED LIBRARY

*Illustrations by John Burgoyne*

# CONTENTS

*introduction*

T HE SUMMER BEFORE COLLEGE I SPENT three months in a Land Rover driving from London to Nairobi, over ten thousand miles of potholes and the famous English rock-hard suspension. (The joke was that if you ran over a penny with a Land Rover, you could feel whether it was tails up or down.) The most memorable part of the trip was the drive through the Sahara Desert, especially the six-hundred-mile trek to Agadez, which was devoid of human life except for a small military outpost that consisted of one small building and half a dozen very hot, unhappy soldiers.

On the second day out, we stopped for lunch and a siesta—we never drove during midday—in a canyon where the thermometer registered just over 120 degrees. I thought that New York City in July was hot, but this was transcendent heat, heat that could make an American teenager immobile and speechless for hours.

The difference between an ordinary hot day and that

canyon in Niger is the difference between home wok cooking and the real thing. To stir-fry properly you need plenty of shimmering, intense heat; enough to caramelize sugars, bring out flavors, and evaporate juices in an instant. The problem is that a wok married to a home stovetop is a lousy partnership, one that provides, at best, moderate heat.

After much work, our test kitchen determined that an American stove requires an American pan, a large nonstick skillet. In addition, we found that sauces don't need cornstarch, most vegetables don't need blanching, and that protein should be a small component in any stir-fry.

This book contains the results of our exhaustive research and testing. The recipes are reliable, easy to prepare, and delicious. Best of all, each stir-fry is a complete meal when served with rice.

We have also published *How to Make a Pie* and *How to Make an American Layer Cake*, and many other titles in this series will soon be available. To order other books, call us at (800) 611-0759. We are also the editors and publishers of *Cook's Illustrated*, a bimonthly publication about American home cooking. For a free trial copy of *Cook's*, call (800) 526-8442.

Christopher P. Kimball
Publisher and Editor
*Cook's Illustrated*

*chapter one*

ろ

# ANATOMY OF A STIR-FRY

T O STIR-FRY PROPERLY YOU NEED plenty of intense heat. The pan must be hot enough to caramelize sugars, deepen flavors, and evaporate unnecessary juices. All this must happen in minutes. The problem for most American cooks is that the Chinese wok and American stovetop are a lousy match that generates moderate heat at best.

Woks are conical because in China they traditionally rest in cylindrical pits containing the fire. Food is cut into small pieces to shorten cooking time, thus conserving fuel. Only one vessel is required for many different cooking methods, including sautéing (stir-frying), steaming, boiling, and deep frying.

Unfortunately, what is practical in China makes no sense in America. A wok was not designed for stovetop cooking, where heat comes only from the bottom. On an American stove, the bottom of the wok gets hot but the sides are only warm. A horizontal heat source requires a horizontal pan. Therefore, for stir-frying at home, we recommend a large skillet, twelve to fourteen inches in diameter, with a nonstick coating.

American stoves necessitate other adjustments. In Chinese cooking, intense flames lick the bottom and sides of a wok, heating the whole surface to extremely high temperatures. Conventional stoves simply don't generate enough British Thermal Units (BTUs) to heat any pan (whether a wok or flat skillet) sufficiently. American cooks must accommodate the lower horsepower on their stoves. Throw everything into the pan at one time and the ingredients will steam and stew, not stir-fry.

One solution is to boil the vegetables first so that they are merely heated through in the pan with the other stir-fry ingredients. We find this precooking to be burdensome and reserve it only for vegetables such as broccoli and cauliflower that require it. We prefer to cut the vegetables quite small and add them to the pan in batches. By adding a small volume of food at a time, the heat in the pan does not dissipate. Slow-cooking vegetables such as carrots and onions go into the pan first, followed by quicker-cooking items such as zucchini and bell peppers. Leafy greens and herbs go in last.

When the vegetables are done, the aromatics (scallions, ginger, and garlic) are briefly cooked and then the seared meat, chicken, seafood, or tofu is added back to the pan along with the sauce. The result is a complete meal, perfect for weeknight dinners, that takes into account the realities of cooking in an American kitchen.

## POINTERS FOR SUCCESS
We uncovered a number of helpful tips and discoveries in our stir-fry testing. Keep these points in mind as you work through the recipes in this book.

### ▪▪ FREEZE, SLICE, AND MARINATE PROTEIN
Most stir-fries start with some sort of protein, either beef, chicken, pork, shrimp, scallops, squid, fish, or tofu. All protein must be cut into bite-size pieces. We find it best to freeze beef, chicken, and pork for an hour or so to make slicing easier. We marinate all protein, once sliced, in a mixture of soy sauce and dry sherry while preparing the vegetables and sauce. Just make sure to drain the protein before stir-frying. If you add the marinating liquid, the protein will stew rather than sear.

**10**

## ▪▪ PROPER RATIO OF PROTEIN TO VEGETABLES

A good stir-fry for four people needs only a three-quarter pound of protein to one and one-half pounds of prepared vegetables. This ratio keeps the stir-fry from becoming too heavy and is more authentic since meat is a luxury used sparingly in China. Serve with plenty of rice (see recipes in chapter six) or over boiled noodles, especially Chinese egg noodles (which resemble linguine) or thin cellophane rice noodles (which look like transparent angel hair pasta).

## ▪▪ COOK IN BATCHES

Most proteins can be cooked in a single batch. The exceptions are flank steak, pork tenderloin, scallops, and squid, which shed a lot of liquid and will stew if cooked all at once. Vegetables, with a few exceptions such as snow peas, must be batched so that no more than one-half pound is added to the pan at one time.

In any case, sear the protein first and then remove it from the pan before cooking the vegetables. Start longer-cooking vegetables, such as onions and carrots, first. With the first batch still in the pan, add medium-cooking vegetables, such as bell peppers and mushrooms, and then finally add fast-cooking leafy greens and fresh herbs. Note that vegetable cooking times will be affected by how they are prepared. For instance, sliced mushrooms will cook more quickly than whole mushrooms. Keep this in mind when deciding in what order to add vegetables to your own stir-fries.

In some cases, you may need to remove cooked vegetables from the pan before adding the next batch. This is especially important if you are cooking large amounts of leafy vegetables that throw off a lot of liquid, such as spinach. Follow the suggestions in individual recipes.

■■ VARY AMOUNT OF OIL BASED ON INGREDIENTS
Some foods, such as shrimp and chicken, will not stick much and can be stir-fried in a minimum of oil, no more than one tablespoon. Other foods, such as fish, eggplant, and mushrooms, tend to soak up oil and may require more. See specific recipes for suggestions.

■■ PRECOOK VEGETABLES ONLY AS NEEDED
We prefer not to precook vegetables, which often adds an unnecessary step. We would rather cut vegetables quite small (no larger than a quarter). However, some vegetables, such as broccoli and cauliflower florets, are difficult to cut this small; they tend to fall apart. Other vegetables, such as asparagus and green beans, may burn on the exterior before cooking through if added raw to a stir-fry. Therefore, we find it is necessary to blanch broccoli and cauliflower florets as well as asparagus and green beans.

12

## ■ ADD AROMATICS AT END

Many stir-fry recipes add the aromatics (scallions, garlic, and ginger) too early, causing them to burn. After cooking the vegetables, we push them to the sides of the pan, add a little oil and the aromatics to the center of the pan, and cook briefly until fragrant but not colored, about ten seconds. To keep the aromatics from burning and becoming harsh-tasting, we then remove the pan from the heat and stir them into the vegetables for twenty seconds.

## ■ VARY AROMATICS AS NEEDED

We find that two tablespoons of chopped scallion whites, one tablespoon of minced garlic, and one tablespoon of minced ginger works well in a basic stir-fry for four. But feel free to adjust these amounts based on personal tastes and other ingredients in the stir-fry. For instance, beef works well with more garlic, and many seafood dishes taste fine with more ginger. To add heat to any stir-fry, add hot red pepper flakes or minced fresh chiles with the aromatics.

## ■ DON'T USE CORNSTARCH IN SAUCES

Once the aromatics have been cooked, it's time to add the cooked protein and the sauce. We find that cornstarch-thickened sauces are often gloppy and thick. Omitting this ingredient produces cleaner-tasting and brighter sauces.

Without cornstarch, it is necessary to keep the amount of sauce to a reasonable amount (about one-half cup) that will thicken slightly on its own with a minute or so of cooking.

**USE SUGAR SPARINGLY**

Even sweet sauces, such as sweet-and-sour, should contain a minimum of sugar. Too much Chinese food prepared in this country is overly sweet. A little sugar is authentic (and delicious) in many recipes; a lot of sugar is not.

**READ MASTER RECIPES**

The following Master Recipe for Basic Stir-Fry is the key to understanding the recipes in this book. Read it carefully. The individual stir-fry recipes in Chapters Three, Four, and Five use the master recipe, with specific proteins, vegetables, and sauces plugged in to create delicious meals. Chapter Six contains recipes for a variety of simple sauces as well as several rice preparations. For detailed information on equipment and ingredients, turn to Chapter Two.

♛

*Master Recipe*

# Basic Stir-Fry

➤ **NOTE:** *Figures 1–9, page 18, illustrate the essential steps in this recipe. You may use a regular 12- or 14-inch skillet or a 12-inch Dutch oven in place of the recommended nonstick skillet, but you will need to use slightly more oil. This recipe serves four people.*

| | |
|---|---|
| ¾ | pound meat, seafood, or tofu, cut into small, even pieces |
| 1 | tablespoon soy sauce |
| 1 | tablespoon dry sherry |
| 1 | recipe any sauce from Chapter 6 |
| 2–4 | tablespoons peanut or vegetable oil |
| 1½ | pounds prepared vegetables, cut into small pieces (none bigger than a quarter) and divided into several batches based on cooking times |
| 2 | tablespoons minced scallions, white parts only |
| 1 | tablespoon minced garlic |
| 1 | tablespoon minced fresh gingerroot |

♛

*Master Instructions*

# Basic Stir-Fry

**1.** Toss meat, seafood, or tofu with soy sauce and sherry in medium bowl; set aside and toss once or twice as you work on rest of recipe. Prepare sauce and vegetables; set aside.

**2.** Heat 12- or 14-inch nonstick skillet over high heat for 3 to 4 minutes. (Pan should be so hot you can hold outstretched hand one inch over pan for only three seconds.) Add 1 tablespoon oil (2 tablespoons for fish) and swirl oil so that it evenly coats bottom of pan. Heat oil until it just starts to shimmer and smoke. Check heat with hand as before.

**3.** Drain meat, seafood, or tofu and add to pan. (Add beef, pork, scallops, and squid in two batches.) Stir-fry until seared and about three-quarters cooked, 40 to 60 seconds for fish and scallops; 1 minute for beef, shrimp, and squid; 2 minutes for pork; 2½ minutes for tofu; and 2½ to 3 minutes for chicken. Scrape cooked meat, seafood, or tofu and all liquid into bowl. Cover and keep warm.

**4.** Let pan come back up to temperature, 1 to 2 minutes. When hot, drizzle in 2 teaspoons oil. When oil just starts to smoke, add first batch of long-cooking vegetables. Stir-fry until vegetables are just tender-crisp, 1 to 2 minutes. Leaving first batch in pan, repeat with remaining vegetables, adding 1 teaspoon oil for each batch and cooking each set until crisp-tender, or wilted for leafy greens.

**5.** Clear center of pan and add scallions, garlic, and ginger. Drizzle with ½ teaspoon oil. Mash into pan with back of a spatula. Cook until fragrant but not colored, about 10 seconds. Remove pan from heat and stir scallions, garlic, and ginger into vegetables for 20 seconds.

**6.** Return pan to heat and add cooked meat, seafood, or tofu. Stir in sauce and stir-fry until ingredients are well coated with sauce and sizzling hot, about 1 minute. Serve immediately with rice.

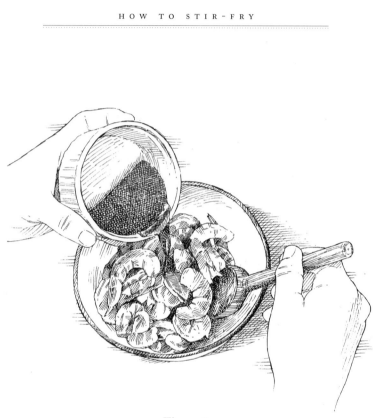

*Figure 1.*
*Toss protein (meat, seafood, or tofu) with soy sauce and*
*dry sherry in a small bowl. Allow to marinate while preparing*
*sauce and vegetables.*

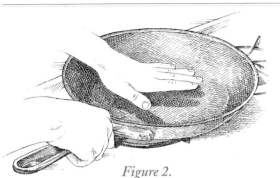

*Figure 2.*
*When ingredients are ready, heat 12- or 14-inch nonstick skillet*
*over high heat for 3 to 4 minutes. Hold hand one inch over pan.*
*When pan is so hot you can keep your hand there for only three*
*seconds, add oil and heat until it just starts to shimmer and smoke.*

*Figure 3.*
*Drain meat, seafood, or tofu and add*
*to hot pan. Cook until seared and three-quarters done*
*and then transfer to bowl. Cover and keep warm.*

*Figure 4.*
*When pan comes back to heat, 1 to 2 minutes, add 2 teaspoons oil.*
*Heat briefly, then add first batch of longer-cooking vegetables.*

*Figure 5.*
*Leaving first batch of vegetables in pan, add additional oil and*
*remaining vegetables in two more batches.*

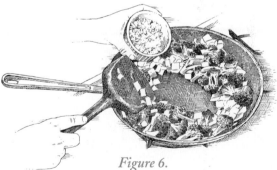

*Figure 6.*
*When all vegetables are crisp-tender, clear center of pan, add*
*scallions, garlic, and ginger, and drizzle with ½ teaspoon oil.*

*Figure 7.*
*Mash scallions, garlic, and ginger into pan with back of spatula.*
*Cook 10 seconds; remove pan from heat and stir scallion*
*mixture into vegetables.*

*Figure 8.*
*Return pan to heat and add cooked meat, seafood, or tofu along*
*with juices in bowl.*

*Figure 9.*
Stir in sauce and stir-fry for a minute or so to coat all ingredients and make sure everything is sizzling hot.

*chapter two*

# EQUIPMENT AND INGREDIENTS

S TIR-FRYING REQUIRES FEW PIECES OF specialized equipment (you may already own them), but there are a number of ingredients that may seem unfamiliar. Here's a brief guide to buying and using the right tools and ingredients.

## TOOLS FOR SUCCESS

### ▪ PLASTIC SPATULA

Chinese cooks use long-handled metal food pushers or shovel spatulas to move food around woks. The same tool works well in a nonstick skillet, although to protect the pan's surface, you should use only plastic or wooden implements. We prefer large shovels with a wide, thin blade and long, heat-resistant handle.

## ▐ NONSTICK SKILLET

We prefer a 12- or 14-inch nonstick skillet for stir-frying. This pan requires a minimum of oil and prevents foods from burning onto the surface as they stir-fry. We tested the major brands of nonstick skillets and particularly liked pans from All-Clad and Calphalon. Both pans are sturdy but not overly heavy. For instance, many enameled cast-iron pans weigh close to five pounds and are hard to maneuver. A pan that weighs about three pounds is much easier to control and still heavy enough to heat evenly. When shopping, make sure the handle is comfortable and preferably heat-resistant. A hollowed-out metal handle or a handle with a removable plastic sheath is ideal.

Our second choice for stir-frying is a regular 12- or 14-inch skillet. Without the nonstick coating, you will need to use slightly more oil. However, this pan will deliver excellent results. Look for the same features (a sturdy but not overly heavy pan with a heat-resistant handle is best) as with a nonstick skillet.

If you do not own a large skillet of any kind, do not substitute a smaller size. A 10-inch skillet is not large enough to accommodate all the ingredients in a stir-fry recipe for four.

The ingredients will steam and stew rather than stir-fry.

A large Dutch oven with a 12-inch base can be used for stir-frying if you do not own a large skillet. It's a bit harder to maneuver this pan (swirling oil and scraping out the cooked protein are easier in a shallow skillet with a handle), but as long as the pan bottom is large enough, a Dutch oven will work fine. As with a regular skillet, you may need to use more oil to keep ingredients from sticking.

### ■ RICE COOKER

A heavy-duty saucepan with a tight-fitting lid is fine for preparing rice. However, if you make rice often, an electric rice cooker may be a wise investment. First of all, rice cookers are foolproof. Just add the right amount of water and rice and walk away. No need to adjust the temperature or check for doneness. An automatic sensor heats the water and then shuts off the cooker when all the water has been absorbed. Best of all, there is no need to time rice perfectly. All electric cookers automatically keep rice steaming hot for hours. Many models also come with nonstick pots that eliminate tedious cleanup.

## STIR-FRY PANTRY

### ■ ASIAN SESAME OIL

Also known as dark or toasted sesame oil, this aromatic

brown oil is used as a seasoning in sauces. Because of its low smoke point, it is not used for cooking. Do not substitute regular sesame oil, which is pressed from untoasted seeds and meant for salad dressings and cooking. Japanese brands of sesame oil are commonly sold in American supermarkets and are generally quite good. Sesame oil tends to go rancid quickly, so store it in a cool cabinet or refrigerate an opened bottle if you will not use it up within a couple of months.

## CHILI PASTE

Sometimes labeled chili sauce, chili paste is a spicy seasoning made with crushed chile peppers, vinegar, and usually garlic. The texture is thick and smooth and the color is bright red. Brands vary from mild to incendiary, so taste before using chili sauce, and adjust as needed. Opened bottles can be refrigerated for many months.

## DRIED HOT RED PEPPER FLAKES

Also called crushed hot red pepper flakes, this pantry staple is a convenient way to add heat to most any stir-fry recipe. We find that adding hot red pepper flakes along with the aromatics (scallions, garlic, and ginger) maximizes their flavor. Note that hot red pepper flakes will lose their punch over time and should be replaced at least twice a year

## ■ DRY SHERRY

We tested various combinations of ingredients for marinating the protein in our stir-fry recipes, including soy sauce, dry sherry, rice wine, chicken stock, sesame oil, cornstarch, and egg whites. We found that a simple mixture of soy sauce and dry sherry provides the best flavor. Rice wine also works well, but since most American cooks are not likely to have this ingredient on hand, our recipes call for dry sherry. Of course, if you have rice wine in the pantry, use an equal amount in place of the sherry.

## ■ SOY SAUCE

Soy sauce is the most important condiment in Asian cooking. Made from equal parts soybeans and roasted grains (usually wheat), plus water and salt, this fermented sauce is an all-purpose condiment that works with many other flavors. Many Americans confuse soy sauce with tamari. Soy sauce is made with wheat, while tamari contains just soybeans, water, and salt. Tamari is generally saltier and darker and better-suited as a dipping sauce (with sushi, for instance) than as a seasoning in cooking.

There are several kinds of soy sauce commonly sold in supermarkets in this country. For the most part, we prefer regular Chinese soy sauce. It's our choice for marinating meat, seafood, or tofu, or for adding a salty, fermented flavor to sauces. However, when using a larger amount of soy sauce, we prefer to use a light or reduced-sodium brand. For instance, a ginger sauce that contains three tablespoons of soy sauce would be too salty if made with a regular, full-sodium sauce. Unless otherwise noted, recipes were tested with regular soy sauce.

## ▓ SZECHWAN PEPPERCORNS

Szechwan peppercorns have a mildly peppery, herbal flavor and aroma. If possible, smell peppercorns before buying them to gauge freshness and intensity. Twigs and tiny leaves will be mixed in with the peppercorns (just pick them out as you use the peppercorns), but there should be a minimum of black seeds. To bring out their flavor, toast peppercorns in a dry skillet until fragrant and then grind them in a coffee mill set aside for spices.

*chapter three*

3

# MEAT AND POULTRY STIR-FRIES

BEEF STIR-FRIES ARE BEST MADE WITH flank steak. It slices thin and stays tender when cooked over high heat. We tried other cuts, such as top round, and found that they become tough when stir-fried. Slightly frozen flank steak is easier to slice thin than meat at room temperature. The same holds true for chicken and pork. An hour in the freezer firms up the texture nicely. Another option is to defrost meat in the refrigerator and slice it while still partially frozen.

Flank steak sheds a fair amount of liquid. To keep the

meat from stewing in its own juices, we prefer to sear flank steak in two batches. When the first batch is nicely browned, scrape out the meat and all juices and transfer them to a small bowl. Add a little more oil and then the second batch of meat to the pan. When that batch is done, add the meat and juices to the bowl, then cover the bowl. Bring the empty skillet back up to temperature and proceed with cooking the vegetables. Each batch of beef will require about one minute of cooking time.

The chicken recipes in this chapter call for boneless, skinless breasts that are cut into ½-inch-wide strips. If you can find boneless, skinless thighs (or want to bone and skin the thighs yourself), go ahead and use this tasty dark meat. Thighs should be cut into 1-inch pieces. Both breast and thigh meat require a fairly long time, at least two and one-half to three minutes, to cook through and brown slightly.

Many traditional stir-fry recipes use ground pork. We prefer lean tenderloin and cut it into long, thin strips that cook in about two minutes. Like flank steak, pork tenderloin can shed a lot of liquid and should be stir-fried in two batches.

# Stir-Fried Beef and Eggplant in Oyster Sauce

➤ NOTE: *If you like, add 1 teaspoon minced fresh chile along with the garlic and ginger. The eggplant must be cooked in two batches to keep the pan from losing heat.*

¾ pound flank steak, sliced thin (*see* figures 10 and 11, page 33)

1 tablespoon soy sauce

1 tablespoon dry sherry

1 recipe Oyster Sauce (*see* page 86)

4–5 tablespoons peanut or vegetable oil

1 medium eggplant (about 1 pound), cut into ¾-inch cubes

1 red bell pepper, cleaned and cut into 3- by ½-inch strips

3 medium scallions, green parts cut into ¼-inch lengths and white parts minced

2 tablespoons minced garlic

1 tablespoon minced fresh gingerroot

⸭ INSTRUCTIONS: Follow Master Recipe instructions for Basic Stir-Fry (*see* page 15), cooking beef in two batches, each in 1 tablespoon oil until seared, about 1 minute. Cook eggplant in two batches, each in 1 tablespoon oil for

1 to 2 minutes. When second batch of eggplant is done, add first batch of eggplant back to pan along with pepper and cook 1 minute. Add scallion greens and cook 15 to 30 seconds.

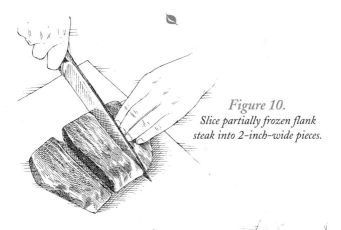

*Figure 10.*
*Slice partially frozen flank*
*steak into 2-inch-wide pieces.*

*Figure 11.*
*Cut each piece of flank steak*
*against the grain into very*
*thin slices.*

# Stir-Fried Beef and Vegetables in Szechwan Chile Sauce

➤ NOTE: *Precook broccoli and cauliflower before stir-frying. Blanch broccoli for 1 to 2 minutes; cauliflower, for 1 minute.*

¾     pound flank steak, sliced thin
      (*see* figures 10 and 11, page 33)

1     tablespoon soy sauce

1     tablespoon dry sherry

1     recipe Szechwan Chile Sauce (*see* page 88)

3-4    tablespoons peanut or vegetable oil

4     cups broccoli florets, blanched until crisp-tender

3     cups cauliflower florets,
      blanched until crisp-tender

1     red bell pepper, cleaned and cut into
      3- by ½-inch strips

2     tablespoons minced scallions, white parts only

2     tablespoons minced garlic

1     tablespoon minced fresh gingerroot

▓ INSTRUCTIONS: Follow Master Recipe instructions for Basic Stir-Fry (*see* page 15), cooking beef in two batches, each in 1 tablespoon oil, until seared, about 1 minute. Add broccoli and cook 1 to 2 minutes. Add cauliflower and cook 1 minute. Add pepper and cook 1 minute.

# Stir-Fried Beef and Snow Peas in Ginger Sauce

➤ **NOTE:** *This classic stir-fry has a clean, bright ginger flavor. Snow peas require so little cooking that one pound may be cooked in a single batch.*

| | |
|---|---|
| ¾ | pound flank steak, sliced thin (*see* figures 10 and 11, page 33) |
| 1 | tablespoon soy sauce |
| 1 | tablespoon dry sherry |
| 1 | recipe Ginger Sauce (*see* page 83) |
| 3 | tablespoons peanut or vegetable oil |
| 1¼ | pounds snow peas, stringed |
| 1 | 8-ounce can sliced bamboo shoots in water, drained |
| 2 | tablespoons minced scallions, white parts only |
| 1 | tablespoon minced garlic |
| 1 | tablespoon minced fresh gingerroot |

▓ **INSTRUCTIONS:** Follow Master Recipe instructions for Basic Stir-Fry (*see* page 15), cooking beef in two batches, each in 1 tablespoon oil until seared, about 1 minute. Add snow peas and cook 1 minute. Add bamboo shoots and cook 30 seconds.

# Stir-Fried Chicken, Pineapple, and Red Onion in Sweet-and-Sour Sauce

➤ NOTE: *Cut fresh or canned pineapple rings into ½–inch-thick triangles that measure about 1 inch long per side.*

| | |
|---|---|
| ¾ | pound boneless, skinless chicken breast, cut into uniform pieces (*see* figures 12-14, page 37) |
| 1 | tablespoon soy sauce |
| 1 | tablespoon dry sherry |
| 1 | recipe Sweet-and-Sour Sauce (*see* page 81) |
| 2–3 | tablespoons peanut or vegetable oil |
| 2 | small red onions, peeled and cut into thin wedges |
| 1 | 20-ounce can pineapple rings in juice, drained, or 2 cups fresh pineapple cut into wedges |
| 3 | medium scallions, green parts cut into ¼-inch lengths and white parts minced |
| 1 | tablespoon minced garlic |
| 1 | tablespoon minced fresh gingerroot |

▓ INSTRUCTIONS: Follow Master Recipe instructions for Basic Stir-Fry (*see* page 15), cooking chicken in 1 tablespoon oil until slightly browned, 2½ to 3 minutes. Add onion and cook 1 to 2 minutes. Add pineapple and cook 1 minute. Add scallion greens and cook 15 to 30 seconds.

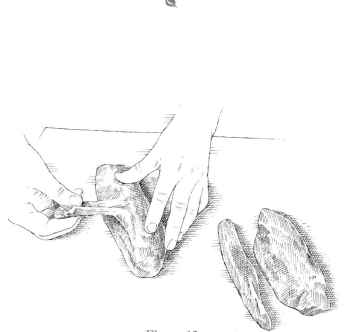

*Figure 12.*
*To produce uniform pieces of chicken, separate tenderloins from partially frozen skinless, boneless breasts.*

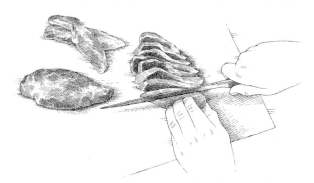

*Figure 13.*
*Slice breasts across the grain into ½-inch-wide strips that are*
*1½ to 2 inches long. Center pieces need to be cut in half so that*
*they are approximately the same length as end pieces.*

*Figure 14.*
*Cut tenderloins on the diagonal to produce pieces about*
*the same size as the strips of breast meat.*

# Stir-Fried Chicken, Celery, and Peanuts in Szechwan Chile Sauce

➤ NOTE: *Salted or natural peanuts may be used in this recipe.*

| | |
|---|---|
| ¾ | pound boneless, skinless chicken breast, cut into uniform pieces (*see* figures 12-14, page 37) |
| 1 | tablespoon soy sauce |
| 1 | tablespoon dry sherry |
| 1 | recipe Szechwan Chile Sauce (*see* page 88) |
| 2-3 | tablespoons peanut or vegetable oil |
| 8 | celery stalks, sliced thin on the bias (*see* figure 15, page 40) |
| 2 | tablespoons minced scallions, white parts only |
| 1 | tablespoon minced garlic |
| 1 | tablespoon minced fresh gingerroot |
| ½ | cup peanuts |

∷ INSTRUCTIONS: Follow Master Recipe instructions for Basic Stir-Fry (*see* page 15), cooking chicken in 1 tablespoon oil until slightly browned, 2½ to 3 minutes. Cook celery in two batches, each for 1½ to 2 minutes. Add first batch of celery back to pan before adding scallions, garlic, and ginger. Add peanuts with cooked chicken and sauce.

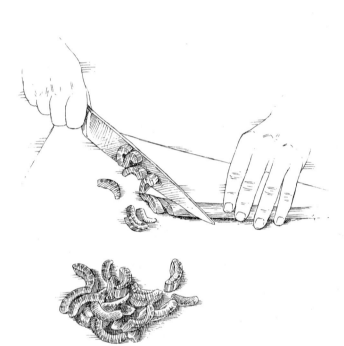

*Figure 15.*
*To cut long, thin vegetables such as celery on the bias, hold knife*
*at a 45-degree to vegetable as you slice.*

# Stir-Fried Chicken and Bok Choy in Ginger Sauce

➤ NOTE: *The white bok choy stalks require more cooking time than the greens, so separate the stalks and leaves before slicing them.*

| | |
|---|---|
| ¾ | pound boneless, skinless chicken breast, cut into uniform pieces (*see* figures 12-14, page 37) |
| 1 | tablespoon soy sauce |
| 1 | tablespoon dry sherry |
| 1 | recipe Ginger Sauce (*see* page 83) |
| 3 | tablespoons peanut or vegetable oil |
| 1 | pound bok choy, stalks and greens separated and sliced thin (*see* figures 16-18, page 42) |
| 1 | red bell pepper, cleaned and cut into 3- by ½-inch strips |
| 2 | tablespoons minced scallions, white parts only |
| 1 | tablespoon minced garlic |
| 1 | tablespoon minced fresh gingerroot |

❖ INSTRUCTIONS: Follow Master Recipe instructions for Basic Stir-Fry (*see* page 15), cooking chicken in 1 table-spoon oil until slightly browned, 2½ to 3 minutes. Add bok choy stalks and cook 1 to 2 minutes. Add pepper and cook 30 to 60 seconds. Add bok choy greens and cook 15 to 30 seconds.

41

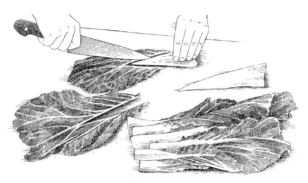

*Figure 16.*
*Cut the leafy green portions of the bok choy away from*
*the white stalks.*

*Figure 17.*
*Cut each white stalk in half lengthwise and then crosswise*
*into thin strips.*

42

*Figure 18.*
*Stack the leafy greens and then slice them crosswise into thin*
*strips. Keep the sliced stalks and leaves separate.*

# Stir-Fried Chicken and Broccoli in Coconut Curry Sauce

➤ NOTE: *Blanch broccoli until crisp-tender (about two minutes) before proceeding with stir-fry recipe.*

| | |
|---|---|
| ¾ | pound boneless, skinless chicken breast, cut into uniform pieces (*see* figures 12-14, page 37) |
| 1 | tablespoon soy sauce |
| 1 | tablespoon dry sherry |
| 1 | recipe Coconut Curry Sauce (*see* page 87) |
| 2–3 | tablespoons peanut or vegetable oil |
| 1 | small onion, cut into 1-inch cubes |
| 1½ | pounds broccoli, florets broken into bite-size pieces; stems trimmed, peeled, and cut into ¼-inch dice |
| 1 | yellow bell pepper, cleaned and cut into 3- by ½-inch strips |
| 2 | tablespoons minced scallions, white parts only |
| ½ | tablespoon minced garlic |
| 1 | tablespoon minced fresh gingerroot |

▪▪ INSTRUCTIONS: Follow Master Recipe instructions for Basic Stir-Fry (*see* page 15), cooking chicken in 1 tablespoon oil until browned, 2½ to 3 minutes. Add onion and cook 2 minutes. Add broccoli and cook 1 minute. Add pepper and cook 1 minute.

# Stir-Fried Pork and Red Cabbage in Hot-and-Sour Sauce

➤ NOTE: *To finely shred cabbage, cut cored quarters crosswise into ¼-inch-wide strips.*

| | |
|---|---|
| ¾ | pound pork tenderloin, trimmed of fat and shredded (*see* figures 19 and 20, page 46) |
| 1 | tablespoon soy sauce |
| 1 | tablespoon dry sherry |
| 1 | recipe Hot-and-Sour Sauce (*see* page 78) |
| 3–4 | tablespoons peanut or vegetable oil |
| ¾ | medium red cabbage, cored and shredded (about 9 cups) |
| 1 | medium carrot, peeled and julienned |
| 2 | tablespoons minced scallions, white parts only |
| 1 | tablespoon minced garlic |
| 1 | tablespoon minced fresh gingerroot |

▋ INSTRUCTIONS: Follow Master Recipe instructions for Basic Stir-Fry (*see* page 15), cooking pork in two batches, each in 1 tablespoon oil until seared, about 2 minutes. Cook cabbage in two batches, each for 1½ minutes. When second batch is done, add first batch of cabbage back to pan along with carrot and cook 2 minutes.

*Figure 19.*
To shred the pork, freeze the tenderloin until firm. Cut the tenderloin crosswise into ⅓-inch-thick medallions.

*Figure 20.*
*Slice each medallion into ⅓-inch-wide strips.*

*chapter four*

❧

# SEAFOOD STIR-FRIES

FRESH SEAFOOD WORKS WELL WITH A variety of flavors and is well-suited to stir-fries. Shrimp, scallops, and squid are all good choices because they cook quickly. Buy medium-sized shrimp, which can be left whole in stir-fries. Choose either fresh (which has almost always been frozen and then defrosted at the store) or frozen shrimp. Shrimp may be stir-fried in the shell, but they are easier to eat when shelled (and deveined if necessary) before cooking. Shrimp should be stir-fried until bright pink, about one minute.

Scallops and squid shed a lot of water when stir-fried and should be cooked in batches to keep them from stewing in their own juices. If you can find good-quality bay scallops, use them whole in stir-fries. Otherwise, select sea scallops and cut them into 1-inch pieces. With either variety, remove the tendon that is attached to the side of each scallop. It becomes unpleasantly tough when cooked. Scallops will cook in just forty to sixty seconds. For optimum browning on the outside, turn scallops only once when stir-frying them.

Whole squid, either fresh or frozen, may be purchased cleaned at many fish markets. The tentacles may be stir-fried as is, while the bodies should be cut crosswise into ½-inch rings. Uncleaned squid is sold in many markets, and is considerably cheaper. *See* figures 32 through 36, page 63, for instructions on cleaning squid. Do not cook squid for more than one minute, or you risk toughening it.

When choosing fish for a stir-fry, we prefer a mild-tasting but firm white fish such as sea bass. Thin fillets, such as sole or flounder, will fall apart. We find that oily fish, such as tuna or salmon, taste too distinctive to blend well with many sauces. Our preferred choice is skinned sea bass fillets that are cut into cubes. They will not disintegrate when stir-fried and are mild enough to work with powerful flavors such as ginger, garlic, and chiles. Cod also can be prepared in this fashion. Cubed fish will brown extremely quickly, in no more than forty to sixty seconds.

## Stir-Fried Shrimp and Water Chestnuts in Hot-and-Sour Sauce

➤ NOTE: *Celery and water chestnuts add crunch to this classic stir-fry. You may use either salted or natural cashews.*

| | |
|---|---|
| 1 | pound medium shrimp, peeled and deveined (*see* figures 21-24, page 51) |
| 1 | tablespoon soy sauce |
| 1 | tablespoon dry sherry |
| 1 | recipe Hot-and-Sour Sauce (*see* page 78) |
| 2–3 | tablespoons peanut or vegetable oil |
| 3 | celery stalks, sliced thin on the bias (*see* figure 15, page 40) |
| 2 | 8-ounce cans whole water chestnuts, drained and halved crosswise |
| 2 | tablespoons minced scallions, white parts only |
| 1 | tablespoon minced garlic |
| 1 | tablespoon minced fresh gingerroot |
| ½ | cup cashews |

▓ INSTRUCTIONS: Follow Master Recipe instructions for Basic Stir-Fry (*see* page 15), cooking shrimp in 1 tablespoon oil until bright pink, about 1 minute. Add celery and cook 1 minute. Add water chestnuts and cook 1 minute. Add cashews with cooked shrimp and sauce.

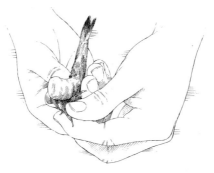

*Figure 21.*
*To peel and devein shrimp, start with shrimp in one hand with legs facing up. Grab as many of the legs as you can with your other hand and peel downward. Moving your thumb toward the tail, continue to peel. With most shrimp you will be able to loosen much of the shell in one piece.*

*Figure 22.*
*Pinch the tail with one hand and gently pull the body away from the tail. The tail meat will come out easily.*

**51**

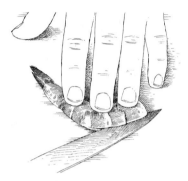

*Figure 23.*
*If the vein that runs along the back of each shrimp is thick and black, we prefer to remove it. If the vein is thin and opaque, we leave it in. To devein shrimp, use a sharp knife to make a slit about ⅛ inch deep along length of back.*

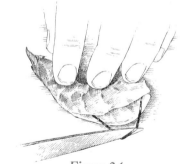

*Figure 24.*
*Lift out the vein with the tip of a knife and discard.*

## Stir-Fried Shrimp, Scallions, and Peppers in Garlic Sauce

➤ NOTE: *Scallions are used as a vegetable in this recipe. You will need four or five bunches, about ¾ pound.*

| | |
|---|---|
| 1 | pound medium shrimp, peeled and deveined (*see* figures 21-24, page 51) |
| 1 | tablespoon soy sauce |
| 1 | tablespoon dry sherry |
| 1 | recipe Garlic Sauce (*see* page 79) |
| 2–3 | tablespoons peanut or vegetable oil |
| 1 | cup scallion whites, sliced into 1-inch pieces |
| 2 | medium red bell peppers, cleaned and cut into 1-inch cubes |
| 1½ | cups scallion greens, sliced into ½-inch pieces |
| 2 | tablespoons minced scallions, white parts only |
| 1 | tablespoon minced garlic |
| 1 | tablespoon minced fresh gingerroot |

⁚⁚ INSTRUCTIONS: Follow Master Recipe instructions for Basic Stir-Fry (*see* page 15), cooking shrimp in 1 tablespoon oil until bright pink, about 1 minute. Add sliced scallion whites and cook 1 to 2 minutes. Add peppers and cook 1 minute. Add scallion greens and cook 30 seconds.

# Stir-Fried Shrimp and Fennel in Spicy Tangerine Sauce

➤ NOTE: *Fennel is not traditional in Chinese stir-fries but softens nicely and complements the sweetness in the shrimp.*

| | |
|--|--|
| 1 | pound medium shrimp, peeled and deveined (*see* figures 21-24, page 51) |
| 1 | tablespoon soy sauce |
| 1 | tablespoon dry sherry |
| 1 | recipe Spicy Tangerine Sauce (*see* page 89) |
| 2–3 | tablespoons peanut or vegetable oil |
| 2 | medium fennel bulbs, sliced thin (*see* figures 25-28, page 55) |
| 1 | red bell pepper, cleaned and cut into ½-inch cubes |
| 3 | medium scallions, green parts cut into ¼-inch lengths and white parts minced |
| ¾ | cup tightly packed stemmed fresh basil leaves |
| 1 | tablespoon minced garlic |
| 1 | tablespoon minced fresh gingerroot |

**INSTRUCTIONS:** Follow Master Recipe instructions for Basic Stir-Fry (*see* page 15), cooking shrimp in 1 tablespoon oil until bright pink, about 1 minute. Add fennel and cook 1½ minutes. Add pepper and cook 30 seconds. Add scallion greens and basil and cook 15 seconds.

*Figure 25.*
*To prepare fennel, trim fronds and stems. Trim a very thin slice*
*from the base and remove any tough or blemished outer layers*
*from the bulb.*

*Figure 26.*
*Cut the bulb in half through the base. Use a small, sharp knife to*
*remove the pyramid-shaped piece of the core in each half.*

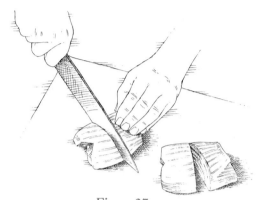

*Figure 27.*
*Lay cored fennel half on a work surface and cut in half crosswise.*

*Figure 28.*
*Cut fennel pieces into ¼-inch-thick strips.*

# Stir-Fried Sea Bass and Vegetables in Spicy Tomato Sauce

➤ NOTE: *For this recipe, cut vegetables into very thin strips that resemble match-sticks or confetti (see figures 29 and 30, page 58).*

| | |
|---|---|
| ¾ | pound skinned sea bass fillet, cut into 1-inch cubes |
| 1 | tablespoon soy sauce |
| 1 | tablespoon dry sherry |
| 1 | recipe Spicy Tomato Sauce (*see* page 80) |
| 3–4 | tablespoons peanut or vegetable oil |
| 2 | medium carrots, peeled and julienned |
| 1 | medium zucchini, julienned |
| 1 | medium yellow summer squash, julienned |
| ½ | medium Napa cabbage (about ½ pound), shredded |
| 2 | tablespoons minced scallions, white parts only |
| 1 | tablespoon minced garlic |
| 2 | tablespoons minced fresh gingerroot |

░ INSTRUCTIONS: Follow Master Recipe instructions for Basic Stir-Fry (*see* page 15), cooking fish in 2 tablespoons oil until lightly browned, 40 to 60 seconds. Add carrots and cook 1 minute. Add zucchini and squash and cook 15 seconds. Add cabbage and cook 15 seconds.

*Figure 29.*
*Long vegetables such as carrots, zucchini, and summer squash*
*can be cut into thin julienned strips (also called matchsticks) that*
*cook quickly. Start by slicing the vegetables on the bias into rounds.*

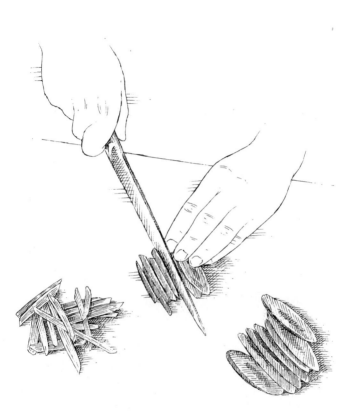

*Figure 30.*
Fan out the vegetable rounds and cut them into strips that measure about 2 inches long and ¼ inch thick.

# Stir-Fried Scallops and Asparagus in Lemon Sauce

➤ **NOTE**: *Use whole bay scallops or sea scallops cut into 1-inch pieces for this dish, which is fairly subtle and benefits from the addition of salt and pepper just before serving. Asparagus blanched for four minutes will cook evenly in a single batch in this dish.*

| | |
|---|---|
| ¾ | pound scallops, tendons removed (*see* figure 31, page 61) and cut if necessary |
| 1 | tablespoon soy sauce |
| 1 | tablespoon dry sherry |
| 1 | recipe Lemon Sauce (*see* page 90) |
| 2 | pounds asparagus, ends snapped off, sliced on the bias into 2-inch pieces, and blanched until crisp-tender |
| 3–4 | tablespoons peanut or vegetable oil |
| 2 | tablespoons minced scallions, white parts only |
| 1 | tablespoon minced garlic |
| 1 | tablespoon minced fresh gingerroot |
| ¼ | cup chopped fresh parsley leaves |
| | Salt and freshly ground black pepper |

▓ **INSTRUCTIONS**: Follow Master Recipe instructions for Basic Stir-Fry (*see* page 15), cooking scallops in two batches, each in 1 tablespoon oil, until opaque, 40 to 60 seconds. To achieve a nicely browned exterior, turn scallops only once while stir-frying. Add asparagus and cook 1½ minutes. Add parsley with cooked scallops and sauce. Season with salt and pepper to taste just before serving.

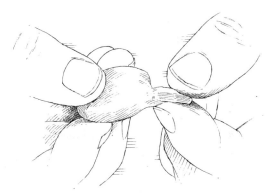

*Figure 31.*
*The small, rough-textured, crescent-shaped muscle that attaches the scallop to the shell will toughen during cooking and should be removed when preparing scallops.*

# Stir-Fried Squid
# in Black Bean Sauce

➤ NOTE: *If you can, buy cleaned squid and simply cut it into ½-inch rings. Otherwise, buy 1½ pounds uncleaned squid and use the instructions in figures 32–36, page 63, to clean it yourself.*

| | |
|---|---|
| ¾ | pound cleaned squid, cut into ½-inch rings (*see* figure 37, page 67) |
| 1 | tablespoon soy sauce |
| 1 | tablespoon dry sherry |
| 1 | recipe Black Bean Sauce (*see* page 82) |
| 3–4 | tablespoons peanut or vegetable oil |
| 2 | celery stalks, halved lengthwise and sliced thin on the bias (*see* figure 15, page 40) |
| ¼ | pound small shiitake mushrooms, stemmed and left whole (about 2 cups) |
| 1 | medium summer squash, quartered lengthwise and cut crosswise into ½-inch-thick triangles |
| ½ | pound sugar snap peas, stringed (about 3 cups) |
| 2 | tablespoons minced scallions, white parts only |
| 1 | tablespoon minced garlic |
| 1 | tablespoon minced fresh gingerroot |

▓ INSTRUCTIONS: Follow Master Recipe instructions for Basic Stir-Fry (*see* page 15), cooking squid in two batches, each in 1 tablespoon oil, until opaque, about 1 minute. Add celery and cook 1½ minutes. Add mushrooms and cook 1 minute. Add squash and cook 1 minute. Add peas and cook 30 to 60 seconds.

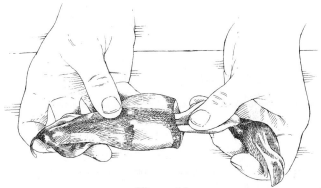

*Figure 32.*
*To clean whole squid, reach into the body with your fingers and grasp as much of the innards as you can. Gently pull out the head and innards.*

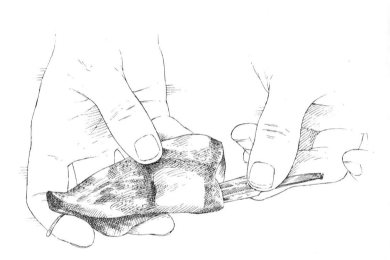

*Figure 33.*
You may have to make a second attempt to remove the hard,
plastic-like quill; it will come out easily once you find it.

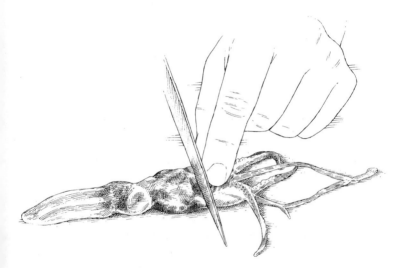

*Figure 34.*
*Cut the tentacles just above the squid's eyes. Be careful of the*
*black ink, which does stain. Discard innards.*

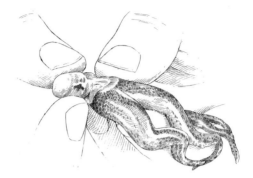

*Figure 35.*
*Check tentacles for an inedible beak. Squeeze out and discard*
*beak if necessary. Reserve tentacles.*

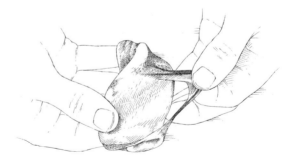

*Figure 36.*
*The thin, membrane-like skin on the squid body is edible but can*
*be easily peeled off for a white appearance.*

*Figure 37.*
*Rinse interior of squid body and then slice it crosswise*
*into ½-inch rings.*

*chapter five*

ॐ

# VEGETARIAN
# STIR-FRIES

TOFU AND/OR VEGETABLES CAN BE used to make meatless stir-fries. Tofu adds a protein element and absorbs the flavors of the sauce well. Stir-frying is a good match for tofu because it browns the tofu cubes and gives them a pleasantly crisp exterior.

We find that firm tofu (rather than soft or silken varieties) holds up best when stir-fried. Like dairy products, tofu is perishable and should be kept well chilled to maximize its shelf-life. We prefer to use tofu within a day or two of its purchase. If you want to keep the tofu for several days, open the package when you get it home from the market and refrigerate the tofu in fresh water. Change the water daily to keep the tofu fresh. Any hints of sourness and the tofu is past its prime.

When ready to stir-fry, drain the tofu and pat it dry with paper towels. We cut tofu into 1-inch cubes to speed cooking. To promote caramelization on the exterior, we turn the tofu as little as possible, no more than two or three times, as it sears. Tofu is hard to overcook, so let it brown for a total of two and one-half minutes.

Tofu is quite bland and we prefer it when paired with very flavorful sauces like those made with fermented black beans or chiles and cider vinegar.

In addition to two tofu recipes, this chapter contains four simple vegetable preparations that can be served as side dishes with a Western meal or as part of a multicourse Chinese meal. These dishes are especially quick to prepare and require a minimum of ingredients. There is also no need to marinate any ingredients in these recipes. We find that two of these dishes benefit from a little seasoning with salt just before serving.

# Stir-Fried Tofu and Two Peppers in Black Bean Sauce

➤ **NOTE:** *Use any combination of red, orange, and yellow bell peppers. Avoid green peppers, which will taste bitter in this dish.*

| | |
|---|---|
| ¾ | pound firm tofu, drained and cut into 1-inch cubes |
| 1 | tablespoon soy sauce |
| 1 | tablespoon dry sherry |
| 1 | recipe Black Bean Sauce (*see* page 82) |
| 2–3 | tablespoons peanut or vegetable oil |
| 4 | bell peppers, cleaned and cut into 3- by ½-inch strips |
| 3 | medium scallions, green parts cut into ¼-inch lengths and whites parts minced |
| 1 | tablespoon minced garlic |
| 1 | tablespoon minced fresh gingerroot |

▓ **INSTRUCTIONS:** Follow Master Recipe instructions for Basic Stir-Fry (*see* page 15), cooking tofu in 1 table-spoon oil until browned on all sides, about 2½ minutes. Cook peppers in two batches, each for about 1½ minutes. When second batch of peppers is done, add first batch of peppers back to pan along with scallion greens and cook 15 to 30 seconds.

**70**

# Stir-Fried Tofu and Vegetables in Hot-and-Sour Sauce

➤ NOTE: *Crunchy sugar snap peas are a good foil for tender tofu. Caramelized red onions add a sweet element.*

| | |
|---|---|
| ¾ | pound firm tofu, drained and cut into 1-inch cubes |
| 1 | tablespoon soy sauce |
| 1 | tablespoon dry sherry |
| 1 | recipe Hot-and-Sour Sauce (*see* page 78) |
| 2–3 | tablespoons peanut or vegetable oil |
| 1 | medium red onion, peeled, quartered, and cut crosswise into ¼-inch slices |
| 1 | pound sugar snap peas, stringed |
| 2 | tablespoons minced scallions, white parts only |
| 1 | tablespoon minced garlic |
| 1 | tablespoon minced fresh gingerroot |

▌ INSTRUCTIONS: Follow Master Recipe instructions for Basic Stir-Fry (*see* page 15), cooking tofu in 1 tablespoon oil until browned on all sides, about 2½ minutes. Add onion and cook 2 minutes. Add peas and cook 2 minutes.

# Stir-Fried Spinach in Ginger Sauce

➤ NOTE: *Serve this stir-fry as a side dish with a roast or as part of a traditional Chinese meal.*

| | |
|---|---|
| 1 | recipe Ginger Sauce (*see* page 83) |
| 2–3 | tablespoons peanut or vegetable oil |
| 2 | pounds stemmed spinach leaves, washed and thoroughly dried |
| 2 | tablespoons minced scallions, white parts only |
| 1 | tablespoon minced garlic |
| 1 | tablespoon minced fresh gingerroot |

▚ INSTRUCTIONS: Follow Master Recipe instructions for Basic Stir-Fry (*see* page 15), cooking spinach in four or five batches, turning leaves often with tongs and adding more oil as needed, until just wilted, 45 to 60 seconds. Transfer each batch to colander-lined bowl before adding the next. Cook aromatics, then add drained spinach back to pan with sauce and heat through.

# Stir-Fried Green Beans
# in Spicy Tomato Sauce

➤ **NOTE:** *The green beans should be blanched for about five minutes before being stir-fried.*

| | |
|---|---|
| 1 | recipe Spicy Tomato Sauce (*see* page 80) |
| 1 | tablespoon peanut or vegetable oil |
| 2 | pounds green beans, stringed, and blanched until crisp-tender |
| 2 | tablespoons minced scallions, white parts only |
| 1 | tablespoon minced garlic |
| 1 | tablespoon minced fresh gingerroot |
| | Salt |

**INSTRUCTIONS:** Follow Master Recipe instructions for Basic Stir-Fry (*see* page 15), cooking beans in 2 teaspoons oil, turning them often with tongs, until heated through, about 2 minutes. Season beans with salt to taste just before serving.

# Stir-Fried Asparagus and Basil in Spicy Tangerine Sauce

➤ NOTE: *Three pounds of asparagus should yield about two pounds when the ends are removed. Blanch trimmed spears for about four minutes.*

| | |
|---|---|
| 1 | recipe Spicy Tangerine Sauce (*see* page 89) |
| 1–2 | tablespoons peanut or vegetable oil |
| 3 | pounds medium asparagus, ends snapped off, halved crosswise, and blanched until crisp-tender |
| ½ | cup tightly packed fresh basil leaves, chopped |
| 2 | tablespoons minced scallions, white parts only |
| 1 | tablespoon minced garlic |
| 1 | tablespoon minced fresh gingerroot |
| | Salt |

▪▪ INSTRUCTIONS: Follow Master Recipe instructions for Basic Stir-Fry (*see* page 15), cooking asparagus in 1 tablespoon oil, turning spears often with tongs, until heated through, about 2 minutes. Add basil and cook 15 seconds. Season with salt to taste just before serving.

# Stir-Fried Snow Peas and Shiitake Mushrooms in Garlic Sauce

➤ NOTE: *We like shiitake mushrooms in this recipe, although other flavorful mushrooms will work just fine. Light brown cremini mushrooms are a good substitute. Unlike the tough, woody stems on shiitakes, the stems on creminis need only be trimmed.*

| | |
|---|---|
| 1 | recipe Garlic Sauce (*see* page 79) |
| 2 | tablespoons peanut or vegetable oil |
| 1 | pound shiitake mushrooms, stemmed and sliced |
| 1 | pound snow peas, stringed |
| 2 | tablespoons minced scallions, white parts only |
| 1 | tablespoon minced garlic |
| 1 | tablespoon minced fresh gingerroot |

▓ INSTRUCTIONS: Follow Master Recipe instructions for Basic Stir-Fry (*see* page 15), cooking mushrooms in two batches, each in 1 tablespoon oil until golden, about 2 minutes. When second batch is done, add first batch of mushrooms to pan along with snow peas and cook 1 minute.

*chapter six*

SAUCES AND
RICE

STRONGLY FLAVORED SAUCES ARE THE KEY to vibrant stir-fries. In our testing, we found that cornstarch makes sauces thick and gloppy. We prefer the cleaner flavor and texture of sauces made without any thickener. A half cup of sauce (all of the following recipes yield this amount) will nicely coat the ingredients in our standard stir-fry without being too liquid. We have made a specific sauce suggestion for each stir-fry, but feel free to create your own combinations of sauce, vegetables, and protein.

The chapter ends with three rice recipes—traditional sticky Chinese white rice, fluffy American-style white rice, and brown rice. The white rice recipes start with the same basic ingredients (rice, water, and salt) but rely on different cooking techniques to produce different results.

For sticky rice, bring the rice, water, and salt to a boil in a saucepan and simmer until the water level drops below the top of the rice. Then lower the heat and cover the pan. After about fifteen minutes, the rice emerges tender and sticky in nice clumps, perfect for picking up with chopsticks.

American-style fluffy white rice is better suited to eating with a fork. Sauté the rice in a little oil to bring out its flavor and then simmer it in a covered saucepan until all the water is absorbed. Then remove the rice from the heat and let it stand to finish cooking. Just before serving, fluff the rice with a fork to separate the grains. This rice tastes nutty from the toasting, while sticky rice has a cleaner flavor.

If you prefer brown rice, we recommend a rice cooker or a two-step cooking method that involves boiling the rice in abundant water until it is almost tender, then steaming it to finish the cooking process and dry out the grains. Because brown rice requires so much time to cook (40 to 45 minutes), we find that it cannot be reliably made in a covered saucepan without running a high risk of scorching.

Each of the following rice recipes yields six cups, a generous amount for four people that follows the Chinese custom of "stretching" a stir-fry by serving it with plenty of rice.

# Hot-and-Sour Sauce

➤ NOTE: *For a spicier sauce, increase the chile to 2 tablespoons or more, if desired.*

| | |
|---|---|
| 3 | tablespoons cider vinegar |
| 1 | tablespoon chicken stock |
| 1 | tablespoon soy sauce |
| 2 | teaspoons sugar |
| 1½ | tablespoons minced jalapeño or other fresh chile |

**INSTRUCTIONS:**

**1.** Combine all ingredients except jalapeño in small bowl and set aside.

**2.** Add jalapeño to stir-fry along with scallions, garlic, and ginger.

# Garlic Sauce

➤ NOTE: *This sauce adds a rich garlic aroma to beef or seafood but does not overpower other ingredients. Adjust the heat as desired.*

| | |
|---|---|
| 3 | tablespoons light soy sauce |
| 4 | teaspoons dry sherry |
| 1 | tablespoon chicken stock |
| 2 | teaspoons soy sauce |
| ½ | teaspoon Asian sesame oil |
| 1 | tablespoon very finely minced garlic |
| ½ | teaspoon sugar |
| ¼ | teaspoon dried hot red pepper flakes |

**INSTRUCTIONS:**

**1.** Combine all ingredients except pepper flakes in small bowl and set aside.

**2.** Add pepper flakes to stir-fry along with scallions, garlic, and ginger.

# Spicy Tomato Sauce

➤ **NOTE:** *This sauce is fairly fiery. Adjust the amount of chili paste for a milder or more incendiary sauce.*

| | |
|---|---|
| 3 | tablespoons tomato paste |
| 2 | tablespoons soy sauce |
| 2 | tablespoons chicken stock |
| 2 | tablespoons dry sherry |
| 2 | teaspoons chili paste |
| ½ | teaspoon Asian sesame oil |
| ½ | teaspoon toasted and ground Szechwan peppercorns |
| ½ | teaspoon sugar |
| ½ | teaspoon dried hot red pepper flakes |

**⁞ INSTRUCTIONS:**

**1.** Combine all ingredients except pepper flakes in small bowl and set aside.

**2.** Add pepper flakes to stir-fry along with scallions, garlic, and ginger.

# Sweet-and-Sour Sauce

➤ NOTE: *Pineapple juice can be used in this recipe instead of orange juice if desired. It's especially appropriate when using pineapple in the stir-fry. The flavors in this sauce are good with chicken, pork, and seafood.*

|        |                              |
|--------|------------------------------|
| 3      | tablespoons red wine vinegar |
| 3      | tablespoons sugar            |
| 1½     | tablespoons tomato sauce     |
| 1½     | tablespoons orange juice     |
| ¼      | teaspoon salt                |

▋ INSTRUCTIONS: Combine ingredients in small bowl and set aside.

# Black Bean Sauce

➤ **NOTE:** *Chinese fermented black beans are available in Asian food shops. They should be moist and soft to the touch. Don't buy beans that are dried-out or shriveled. High-quality fermented beans should not be overly salty.*

| | |
|---|---|
| 3 | tablespoons dry sherry |
| 2 | tablespoons chicken stock |
| 1 | tablespoon soy sauce |
| 1 | tablespoon Asian sesame oil |
| ½ | teaspoon sugar |
| ¼ | teaspoon freshly ground black pepper |
| 1 | tablespoon Chinese fermented black beans, chopped |

**▪▪ INSTRUCTIONS:**

**1.** Combine all ingredients except beans in small bowl and set aside.

**2.** Add beans to stir-fry along with scallions, garlic, and ginger.

# Ginger Sauce

➤ **NOTE:** *For hints on peeling and mincing ginger, see figures 38–40, page 84.*

| | |
|---|---|
| 3 | tablespoons light soy sauce |
| 2 | tablespoons chicken stock |
| 1 | tablespoon soy sauce |
| 1 | tablespoon dry sherry |
| 3 | tablespoons very finely minced fresh gingerroot |
| ½ | teaspoon sugar |

**INSTRUCTIONS:** Combine ingredients in small bowl and set aside.

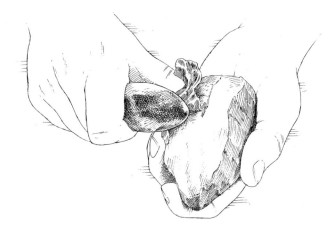

*Figure 38.*
*Use the bowl of a teaspoon to scrape off the knotty skin from a knob of ginger.*

*Figure 39.*
*To mince ginger by hand, slice peeled ginger into thin rounds,*
*then fan rounds out and cut them into thin matchsticks.*

*Figure 40.*
*Chop matchsticks crosswise into fine mince. Peeled ginger may also*
*be cut into small cubes and then crushed in a standard garlic press.*

# Oyster Sauce

➤ **NOTE:** *As the name suggests, oyster sauce is made from fermented oysters, along with salt and spices. The flavor is not overly fishy but is quite salty, so a little goes a long way. This sauce works well with beef and seafood.*

| | |
|---|---|
| 3 | tablespoons dry sherry |
| 2 | tablespoons oyster sauce |
| 1 | tablespoon Asian sesame oil |
| 1 | tablespoon soy sauce |
| ½ | teaspoon sugar |
| ¼ | teaspoon freshly ground black pepper |

**INSTRUCTIONS:** Combine ingredients in small bowl and set aside.

# Coconut Curry Sauce

> NOTE: *Use canned unsweetened coconut milk in this recipe, not sweetened coconut cream. This velvety sauce coats food especially well.*

| | |
|---|---|
| ¼ | cup unsweetened coconut milk |
| 1 | tablespoon dry sherry |
| 1 | tablespoon chicken stock |
| 1½ | teaspoons soy sauce |
| 1½ | teaspoons curry powder |
| ¼ | teaspoon sugar |
| ¼ | teaspoon salt |

INSTRUCTIONS: Combine ingredients in small bowl and set aside.

# Szechwan Chile Sauce

➤ **N O T E :** *This sauce gets its heat from chili paste. Szechwan peppercorns add an aromatic, herbaceous flavor.*

| | |
|---|---|
| 3 | tablespoons dry sherry |
| 1 | tablespoon soy sauce |
| 1 | tablespoon Asian sesame oil |
| 2 | tablespoons chili paste |
| ¼ | teaspoon toasted and ground Szechwan peppercorns |
| ¼ | teaspoon sugar |

**I N S T R U C T I O N S :** Combine ingredients in small bowl and set aside.

# Spicy Tangerine Sauce

➤ **NOTE:** *Three tangerines will provide enough zest for this recipe. An orange may be used instead if desired. Wear rubber gloves when mincing the fresh chile and use the seeds to maximize the heat. For a citrus-flavored sauce without the heat, omit the chile.*

| | |
|---|---|
| 3 | tablespoons dry sherry |
| 1 | tablespoon soy sauce |
| 1 | tablespoon Asian sesame oil |
| 2 | teaspoons red wine vinegar |
| ½ | teaspoon toasted and ground Szechwan peppercorns |
| ¼ | teaspoon sugar |
| ¼ | teaspoon salt |
| 1 | tablespoon minced jalapeño or other fresh chile |
| 1 | tablespoon grated tangerine zest |

▦ **INSTRUCTIONS:**

**1.** Combine all ingredients except jalapeño and tangerine zest in small bowl and set aside.

**2.** Add jalapeño and tangerine zest to stir-fry along with scallions, garlic, and ginger.

# Lemon Sauce

➤ **NOTE:** *One medium lemon will yield enough juice and zest for this recipe.*

| | |
|---|---|
| 3 | tablespoons lemon juice |
| ½ | teaspoon minced lemon zest |
| 2 | tablespoons chicken stock |
| 1 | tablespoon soy sauce |
| 2 | teaspoons sugar |

**INSTRUCTIONS:** Combine ingredients in small bowl and set aside.

# Sticky White Rice

➤ **NOTE:** *This traditional Chinese cooking method yields sticky rice that works well as an accompaniment to a stir-fry, especially if eating with chopsticks.*

| | |
|---|---|
| 2 | cups long-grain white rice |
| 3 | cups water |
| ½ | teaspoon salt |

**INSTRUCTIONS:**

**1.** Place rice, water, and salt in medium saucepan set over medium-high heat. Bring water to boil. Cook, uncovered, until water level drops below top surface of rice and small holes form in rice, about 10 minutes.

**2.** Reduce heat to very low, cover, and cook until rice is tender, about 15 minutes longer.

# Fluffy White Rice

➤ **NOTE:** *We like to toast our rice before adding water. It gives the rice a subtle nutty flavor. Adjust the toasting time to suit your personal tastes. Do not use converted rice in this recipe. If you own a rice cooker, simply add the ingredients to the pot (without toasting the rice) and cook according to the manufacturer's instructions.*

| | |
|---|---|
| 4 | teaspoons vegetable oil |
| 2 | cups long-grain white rice |
| 2¾ | cups water |
| ½ | teaspoon salt |

**▪▪ INSTRUCTIONS:**

**1.** Heat oil in medium saucepan set over medium heat. Add rice; cook, stirring constantly, for 1 to 3 minutes, depending on desired amount of nutty flavor. Add water and salt; bring to boil, swirling pot to blend ingredients.

**2.** Reduce heat to low, cover with tight lid lined with towel, and cook until liquid is absorbed, about 15 minutes.

**3.** Turn off heat; let rice stand on burner, still covered, to finish cooking, about 15 minutes. Fluff with fork and serve.

# Basic Brown Rice

➤ NOTE: *Boiling and then steaming brown rice ensures perfectly cooked grains that do not stick or burn. Use long, medium, or short grain rice in this recipe. If you own a rice cooker, simply add the rice to the pot along with 4½ cups water, 2 teaspoons oil, and ½ teaspoon salt, and cook according to the manufacturer's instructions.*

2    cups brown rice
4    teaspoons vegetable oil
2    teaspoons salt

**INSTRUCTIONS:**

**1.** Bring 3 quarts water to boil in large pot. Stir in rice, oil, and salt. Simmer briskly, uncovered, until rice is almost tender, about 30 minutes.

**2.** Drain rice into steamer basket that fits inside pot. Fill pot with about 1 inch water and return to heat. Place basket of rice in pot, making sure it rests above water level. Cover and steam until tender, 5 to 10 minutes. Scoop rice into bowl, fluff gently with fork, and serve.

# index